WOULD YOU RATHER?
CHRISTMAS
EDITION

RIDDLELAND

☃ TABLE OF CONTENTS ☃

❄ Welcome to the North Pole ❄
(Sort Of)

Hey there!
This isn't just any book; it's your very own backstage pass to the North Pole.
But fair warning: things are a little out of control right now.

The elves are behind on wrapping, the reindeer are doing loop-the-loops over
the gingerbread village, and someone gave the Yeti a kazoo. Let's just say...
Santa could use a break. Or at least a good laugh.

That's where you come in.

Inside this book, you'll find tons of **Would You Rather** questions; each
one crazier (and funnier) than the last. You'll make silly choices, imagine
wild holiday disasters, and maybe even end up with candy canes in your
hair. There are no rules, no wrong answers, and no clean sweaters by the
end of it.

Play it solo. Share it with your family. Shout your answers across the room.
Just promise you'll laugh along the way.

Okay, enough chit-chat.
Grab some cocoa. Take a deep breath.
And whatever you do...
DON'T PRESS THE GLOWING RED BUTTON.

You'll see what we mean.

❄ How To Play ❄

This book is filled with Would You Rather... questions, all with a holiday twist.

Here's how it works:

1. Read the question out loud.
Each one gives you two wild, weird, or downright ridiculous choices.

2. Pick the one you'd rather do.
Would you rather ride a reindeer through a snowstorm... or be in charge of wrapping presents with spaghetti? It's up to you!

3. Play alone or with others.
Take turns, explain your answers, or try to guess what your friends or family would pick. You can even keep score if you want, but mostly, it's just for fun.

4. There are no wrong answers.
Just go with your gut, get silly, and don't be afraid to laugh at the chaos.

That's it!
Now turn the page and get ready to make some of the silliest decisions of your holiday life.

Let the North Pole adventure begin!

Chapter 1

Welcome to the North Pole
·Please Don't Touch Anything·

Welcome to the North Pole! You're the newest honorary helper; lucky you! But whatever you do, don't press the glowing red button. Someone already did... and now the sleigh is flying sideways, the ornament wall is singing opera, and a snowman just tried to order a pizza. Looks like it's going to be one of those days.

Would you rather press a button that blasts candy canes into the sky  one that makes the sleigh spin like a disco ball?

Would you rather taste-test 400 mugs of hot chocolate  inspect every snowball for maximum roundness?

Would you rather steer a runaway gift-wrapping machine  ride a sleigh pulled by lost penguins?

Would you rather get wrapped up and labeled "DO NOT OPEN UNTIL NEXT CHRISTMAS"  or pop out of a giant present in front of the elf choir?

Would you rather wear squeaky elf shoes that shout "LOOK AT ME!"  a hat that sings every time you blink?

Would you rather get splatted
with whipped cream from a clumsy robot

or get blamed for stealing a snowman's nose?

Would you rather
sort Santa's letters while
glitter explodes from
every envelope

open ones that smell like
rotten fruitcake?

Would you rather feed sneezing reindeer  teach snowmen how to cartwheel without melting?

Would you rather trip and set off the jingle bell alarm  sneeze so loud it startles the sleigh reindeer?

Would you rather be chased by frosting-covered elves  by a gingerbread man on roller skates?

Would you rather get zapped by a wall of singing ornaments  get tangled in tinsel that tickles nonstop?

Would you rather paint 5,000 tiny toy noses  polish sleigh bells using only your sleeves?

Would you rather mop up a river
of overflowing hot chocolate

or catch marshmallows that bounce like frogs?

Would you rather
mix up the Naughty and
Nice lists

spill hot chocolate all over
Santa's chimney map?

Would you rather wear elf uniforms made of scratchy candy cane yarn  ride a sled that runs on peppermint burps?

Would you rather get boxed up by mistake and shipped to Antarctica  strung in lights and mistaken for a tree?

Would you rather fold 800 of Santa's itchy sweaters  clean the glitter out of his sock drawer?

Would you rather get sneezed on by a fudge-scented polar bear  licked by a reindeer who thinks you're a candy cane?

Would you rather wake up 500 elves using just a triangle bell  calm them down after a marshmallow explosion?

Would you rather
test Santa's rocket boots

or wear a helmet that blurts out your thoughts?

Would you rather
clean up 900 spilled
jingle bells

OR

chase down a lost parade
of duck-shaped drones?

Would you rather push a sleigh uphill during a snowball stampede  ride it downhill with no brakes?

Would you rather sneeze and set off all the musical toys  hiccup and flash the sleigh lights in Morse code?

Would you rather explain why the cookie printer is full of broccoli  why the hot chocolate machine is burping confetti?

Would you rather work in the bubble-wrap room where everything pops too early  the tinsel tunnel that makes you laugh-snort?

Would you rather wear snowpants that inflate like balloons when you lie  mittens that moo when you clap?

Would you rather get launched into a snowbank by Santa's test trampoline  land in a fudge fountain via parachute?

Would you rather train sleigh-steering squirrels  decode elf complaints written in jellybean symbols?

Would you rather press a button that dumps snow into your boots  one that activates 5,000 whoopee cushions?

Would you rather walk away from the glowing red button  press it again and trigger a blizzard of singing marshmallows in top hats?

Chapter 2:

Santa's Workshop Wipeout

Your first day in the workshop!
How hard could it be? All you had to do was carry one box of
bows… and now the wrapping machine is sneezing, the
glitter cannon won't stop, and Santa's beard got caught in a
conveyor belt. Yeah. This might be your last day, too.

Would you rather chase 400 runaway toy trains headed for Santa's sleigh  rewrap 5,000 gifts unwrapped by the sneezy wrapping machine?

Would you rather fix a nutcracker that won't stop breakdancing  a robot that keeps wrapping lumps of coal as "deluxe presents"?

Would you rather get stuck in the gift tag printer  glitter-blasted by a ribbon blaster that's jammed on "festive firehose"?

Would you rather wrap a trampoline for a family of reindeer  a snowglobe the size of a hot tub?

Would you rather use a singing stapler that only knows "Jingle Bells"  or tape from a dispenser shaped like Rudolph's nose?

Would you rather get boxed up in the "North Pole Emergency Gift kit"  buried under a mountain of squishy snowman plushies that sing carols?

Would you rather sort puzzle pieces using candy cane tongs  build elf bikes while wearing fuzzy oven mitts?

Would you rather deliver presents on stilts shaped like candy canes  roller-skate across jellybean-covered snow?

Would you rather wear wrapping paper as a cape all day  elf boots that shout "WRAPPING ZONE" every time you stop?

Would you rather gift-wrap 1,000 bananas for the reindeer  unroll Santa's ancient scroll of elf jokes, written in Old Sleighish?

Would you rather glue your hand
to the Naughty List

or sit on a singing whoopee cushion
during Santa's workshop tour?

Would you rather
stuff stockings with a giant
peppermint scoop

hang 200 mini socks on a
rotating garland belt?

Would you rather get tangled in 300 feet of blinking holiday lights  wrapped up by the gift wrap robot's octo-arms?

Would you rather refill the mistletoe-launching snow globes  test the toy candy cane launchers... in reverse?

Would you rather deliver a gift to a house guarded by a suspicious caroling goose  one with a peppermint drawbridge?

Would you rather gift-wrap a grumpy rubber chicken dressed like an elf  a cactus that thinks it's a Christmas tree?

Would you rather fold a present shaped like a spaghetti snowman  one that jingles every time you touch it?

Would you rather be chased by
a remote-control toy bulldozer named "Jingles"

or or dodge flying stuffed penguins
during elf plushie testing

Would you rather
build 300 chairs made
entirely of whoopee cushions  paint 200 nutcrackers
with googly eyes?

Would you rather clean up spilled peppermint slime  mop the floor after the marshmallow catapult experiment?

Would you rather press the "Fast Wrapping" button on the toy line  the "Dance Break" button on the elf team?

Would you rather find out you've been gift-wrapping empty boxes  that all your wrapped gifts have barking ornaments inside?

Would you rather wrap presents inside a snowglobe that's slowly filling with jingle bells  on a trampoline during the elves' annual snowball fight?

Would you rather have sticky fingers from candy glue  boots that jingle in slow motion?

Would you rather carry a teddy bear
that shouts "HO HO HUG!" every 10 seconds

or a doll that sneezes glitter on command?

Would you rather
gift-wrap yourself
by accident

deliver a box
that keeps yelling,
"I'M REALLY AN ELF!"

Would you rather wrap 50 bouncing basketball ornaments

10 rubber chickens that honk every time they wiggle?

Would you rather fall into the peppermint frosting vat

sneeze into the snowflake confetti machine right before the elf holiday pageant?

Would you rather explain to Santa why the gift-sorting machine now sorts by smell

why the sleigh's navigation screen spells "UH-OH"?

Would you rather hit the emergency stop button and freeze the madness

quietly tiptoe away and let the toy unicorns explain everything?

Chapter 3

Reindeer Flight School Fiasco

You were doing great at Reindeer Flight School…
until Comet's scarf flew into your face at 300 reindeer-knots.
Now the sleigh's flying sideways, the reindeer are playing tag
midair, and someone hit the emergency glitter chute. This
might be your last flight, and it's not even lunch yet.

Would you rather fly a sleigh pulled by sneezing reindeer  one that only flies in dizzying figure eights?

Would you rather sneeze and trigger emergency glitter jets  hiccup and release a parachute made of tinsel?

Would you rather steer through a candy cane hailstorm that bonks your nose  fly over marshmallow clouds that stick to your goggles?

Would you rather wear reindeer antlers that accidentally launch flares  boots that squeak Jingle Bells every time you blink?

Would you rather bounce off twelve rooftops during landing drills  crash into a hot chocolate fountain shaped like Santa's face?

Would you rather get hit in the face
with a flying fruitcake

or lose your helmet
during sleigh barrel rolls?

Would you rather train a
baby reindeer that follows
you everywhere like a puppy  one that only obeys if you
cluck like a chicken?

Would you rather polish Rudolph's nose with sticky peppermint polish  brush Dasher's tail while he tap dances?

Would you rather ride in a sleigh with reindeer who argue about directions  ones who sing off-key holiday carols at full volume?

Would you rather forget the sleigh's parking brakes  drop the landing checklist into a snowblower?

Would you rather try to guide a reindeer that's scared of snow  one that keeps licking the sleigh windshield?

Would you rather explain why Blitzen is wearing a tutu  admit you taught Cupid to moonwalk?

Would you rather test Santa's GPS
that only speaks penguin

or follow a map drawn in frosting?

Would you rather
carry a sack of gifts that
randomly yells "SURPRISE!"  one that keeps dropping
glitter bombs?

Would you rather fall into a snowdrift of caroling snowmen  get wrapped up in flying gift tags and sticky tape?

Would you rather fly through a tunnel of ticklish tinsel  dodge snowballs thrown by elf instructors with excellent aim?

Would you rather race Prancer through a donut-shaped blizzard  zip through a tunnel made of spinning gingerbread?

Would you rather ride a reindeer that snores mid-flight  one that sneezes peppermint dust every time it flaps its ears?

Would you rather crash into a rooftop trampoline made of jelly  land in Santa's laundry basket?

Would you rather wear sleigh gloves
that smell like fruitcake

or boots that stick to everything
like melted marshmallows?

Would you rather
lose your balance during a
loop-de-loop

steer the sleigh into
a blinking inflatable
snowman?

Would you rather
sit next to a reindeer with
candy cane breath and
no personal space

one who insists
on singing duets?

Would you rather
clean up after a carrot
buffet food fight

explain who taught
Dancer to floss mid-flight?

Would you rather
fly around the North Pole 27
times without landing

stick the landing
but fart loudly
in front of Santa?

Would you rather
collide with a squad of
misfired drone ornaments

a flock of
flying cookies
wearing elf hats?

Would you rather
fly a sleigh that leaves
rainbow glitter trails

one that toots out
"Deck the Halls"
every landing?

Would you rather steer through a blizzard maze shaped like a snowflake  outrun a rogue elf on a peppermint-powered jet sled?

Would you rather forget your sleigh seatbelt just before a flip  be stuck midair with a reindeer who won't stop telling knock-knock jokes?

Would you rather crash the simulator and end up on the Naughty List  be stuck in reindeer school until spring?

Would you rather end the flight now and stick the landing...  press one last button and see what happens when the sleigh sprouts candy wings and takes off for the moon?

Chapter 4:

Elves on Strike!

First, it was one elf demanding longer cookie breaks. Then another wanted candy cane chairs. Now the toy machines have stopped, a frosting banner hangs from the ceiling, and someone dumped sprinkles in Santa's boots. The elves are on strike—and things are getting weirder by the minute.

Would you rather join the elf strike with a giant cookie sign  sneak past the candy cane barricade dressed like a walking present?

Would you rather face a crowd of chanting elves with jellybean slingshots  explain to Santa why his sleigh smells like frosting?

Would you rather sit through a five-hour elf meeting about ribbon rules  be in charge of passing out snacks without spilling the cocoa?

Would you rather wear itchy green tights to support the strike  hold a sign that says "Fruitcake Is My Favorite"?

Would you rather calm down a group of hungry, cranky elves  untangle a huge mess of peppermint lights?

Would you rather refill the marshmallow cocoa machine for 200 grumpy elves  clean up the sticky floors after the cookie protest?

Would you rather chant "More Sprinkles Now!" with the elves  try to distract them by juggling snowballs?

Would you rather lead a reindeer peace parade  bake 300 apology cupcakes shaped like Santa's face?

Would you rather wear a hat that says "Elf Boss" in blinking lights  one that plays "Jingle Bells" every time you move?

Would you rather write an apology using glitter glue  shovel the snow the elves dumped in Santa's sock drawer?

Would you rather eat an entire
protest fruitcake in one bite

or hand out fudge squares to every elf
hiding in the break room?

Would you rather
carry a sign that says
"More Cookies, Less Work!"

try to scrub frosting off
the sleigh roof?

Would you rather build toys using melted gumdrops  glue together 400 candy cane protest whistles?

Would you rather get chased by elf scooters  listen to their new protest song: "We Want Cookies, Not Coal"?

Would you rather trip over the microphone wire during elf karaoke  spill hot chocolate all over the protest list?

Would you rather hand out gummy bear peace treats  get wrapped in tinsel by prankster elves and stuck under the tree?

Would you rather break up an argument between two cookie-loving elves  be the judge in a snowball arm-wrestling match?

Would you rather clean up
a pudding pie mess

or vacuum up glitter that exploded
all over Santa's desk?

Would you rather
get glitter-bombed
during your speech

wear a tutu made of tinsel
until the strike ends?

Would you rather solve a candy cane rhyme puzzle  count every gumdrop from the protest snack pile?

Would you rather take over gift-wrapping duty with sticky mittens  ride a runaway present down the sorting ramp?

Would you rather juggle pudding cups in front of the Elf Cheer-Up Team  wear a sash that says "Elf Hug Boss"?

Would you rather plan elf nap time  lead a karaoke night with the song "We're Not Budging 'Til We Get Cookies"?

Would you rather wash 800 tiny cocoa mugs  polish every jingle bell on the elf uniforms?

Would you rather give a speech
while balancing five candy canes

or sing a strike song called
"No More Fruitcake Fridays"?

Would you rather
accidentally swap
Santa's sleigh bell with
a whoopee cushion

spill glitter ink
on the reindeer
flight map?

Would you rather settle the strike with a cookie-eating contest  lead the elves back to work using a trail of gumdrops?

Would you rather deliver coal to the elf who started the protest  get stuck as the "Snowball Sponge" for a whole week?

Would you rather be taped to a peppermint pole  ride the elf sled while five bouncing penguins pull it?

Would you rather end the strike with a sing-along and marshmallow toast  hit the surprise snowstorm button and turn the workshop into a blizzard dance party?

Chapter 5:

The Naughty List Heist

Someone broke into Santa's private vault last night, and the Naughty List is GONE. Santa's beard is twitching, the elves are panicking, and there's a squirrel in a detective hat pointing fingers at everyone. Now you've been pulled into the case. Your mission? Find the list, avoid glitter booby traps, and try not to land on the list yourself.

Would you rather sneak past a sleeping elf guard wearing bells on your shoes,  tiptoe through a hallway lined with giggling gumdrops?

Would you rather follow a trail of peppermint wrappers that whisper your name  gumdrops that shout "THIEF!" every time you step?

Would you rather hide behind a mountain of stinky reindeer socks  inside a Christmas tree that sneezes ornaments?

Would you rather crawl through a vent that smells like burnt marshmallows  climb through a chimney filled with leftover fruitcake?

Would you rather mime your alibi using candy canes  sing it to the tune of "Deck the Halls" in elf court?

Would you rather wear a detective hat
that's two sizes too big

or carry a candy cane magnifying glass
that keeps melting?

Would you rather
distract a suspicious elf by
juggling jellybeans

by tap dancing
in a tutu made of
wrapping paper?

Would you rather ride a sled through a hallway covered in slippery tinsel  hop across nutcracker helmets without waking them?

Would you rather question a penguin who won't stop rapping about his innocence,  an elf who throws glitter every time he gets nervous?

Would you rather wear a Christmas sweater that says "Definitely Suspicious,"  elf-boots that honk every time you lie?

Would you rather stake out the Naughty List room while sitting on a whoopee-cushion beanbag,  guard the door while eating candy canes that turn your lips green?

Would you rather open a suspicious box that sprays eggnog in your face,  one that plays embarrassing jingles about your underwear?

Would you rather dress up as a giant cookie
to sneak past the gift vault,

or pretend to be a singing wreath
for 20 minutes?

Would you rather
be interrogated by three
nutcrackers with
squeaky voices,

one elf who won't stop
asking about your
snack habits?

Would you rather chase the suspect across an ice floor in fuzzy slippers  bounce on a trampoline made of fruitcake?

Would you rather get stuck in the cocoa machine during your investigation,  be tackled by a nutcracker who thinks you're a candy thief?

Would you rather find the list, but it's been scribbled on with jelly,  accidentally sit on it and get stuck to it for a week?

Would you rather decode a note written in reindeer hoofprints  one made entirely of candy corn and raisins?

Would you rather report your findings to Santa while wearing a beard made of spaghetti,  while hiccuping glitter every time you speak?

Would you rather interrogate a gingerbread man who only
answers in knock-knock jokes,

or a snowman who melts a little
every time you ask a question?

Would you rather
escape the vault by sliding
through a mince-pie tunnel  flying out
the chimney using
balloon-powered
underwear?

Would you rather deliver the recovered list while riding a flamingo in earmuffs,  while being followed by a snowball yelling, "YOU FORGOT ME!"

Would you rather hide the list inside a fruitcake that bites,  tuck it under a reindeer's saddle that keeps slipping off?

Would you rather protect the list by taping it to your belly  hiding it inside a giant rubber duck that honks every 10 seconds?

Would you rather explain to the Elf Council why you ate half the evidence,  why your dog chewed the Naughty List?

Would you rather clear your name by winning a snowball duel  by surviving 10 rounds of "Truth or Dare" in front of a crowd?

Would you rather catch the real thief and get your face on a holiday cereal box,  let them go and have them owe you a mysterious favor?

Would you rather earn a badge that smells like fruitcake  a certificate that sings carols every time someone lies near it?

Would you rather have the case solved but be stuck with a talking ornament sidekick forever,  get promoted to Chief Elf and have to wear a glitter mustache?

Would you rather save Christmas and trip on your way out of the vault in front of everyone,  mess everything up but somehow end up the hero anyway?

Chapter 6:

Gingerbread Gone Wild

What started as a peaceful cookie decorating session
has turned into a full-blown snack uprising.
The gingerbread men are using licorice lassos, frosting tubes
have been turned into frosting cannons, and someone taught
the gumdrops how to throw. You're deep in the sugar zone
now; make your choices carefully... or risk getting frosted.

Would you rather be chased by a gingerbread man with a candy cane jetpack,  one riding a marshmallow goat yelling "FEAR THE FROSTING!"

Would you rather duel a gingerbread pirate who slips on gumdrops every few steps,  negotiate peace with a cookie king who only speaks in marshmallow puns?

Would you rather eat a cookie that turns your voice into a kazoo  one that makes you randomly blurt out cookie trivia every five minutes?

Would you rather wrestle a gingerbread bear in a jelly pit,  dodge a cupcake cannon that keeps misfiring at your face?

Would you rather be stuck in a frosting blizzard inside the mixing room,  trapped in a storage closet with 200 cookies chanting "DECORATE US!"

Would you rather be stuck in a cookie jar that whispers your secrets,  in a fudge tunnel that won't stop playing dramatic music?

Would you rather command a cookie army that takes everything literally,  be best friends with a gingerbread rebel who refuses to wear pants?

Would you rather wear frosting armor that attracts bees,  gumdrop gloves that glue you to whatever you touch?

Would you rather stake out the Naughty List room while sitting on a whoopee-cushion beanbag,  guard the door while eating candy canes that turn your lips green?

Would you rather babysit a cookie who screams every time someone mentions milk,  one who demands to wear a different icing hat every hour?

Would you rather decorate a cookie dinosaur
that keeps trying to sit in your lap

or frost a sugar dragon
that hiccups cinnamon sparks?

Would you rather
snowboard down a hill made
of graham cracker crumbs

ride a cookie sled
through a blizzard of
rainbow sprinkles?

Would you rather get tackled by the gingerbread wrestling team  be the referee for cookie dodgeball using jellybeans?

Would you rather work the cookie assembly line while riding a unicycle  operate the sprinkle machine while blindfolded?

Would you rather crawl through a licorice maze full of sarcastic candy canes,  escape from a room where the walls are slowly closing in... with gumdrops?

Would you rather be covered in frosting from head to toe but win the Cookie Crown,  stay crumb-free but get booed by a room full of gingerbread judges?

Would you rather train a sugar cookie dragon that only listens to polka,  teach a shortbread unicorn how to tap dance?

Would you rather make a Christmas
wreath out of cookie dough

or build a Christmas tree
out of profiteroles?

Would you rather
decorate cupcakes that
explode into glitter sneezes,  pipe frosting
onto donuts that sing
when tickled?

Would you rather play hide-and-seek with a cookie who turns invisible when scared,  tag with a gingerbread ninja who hides in the walls?

Would you rather ice-skate with crackers that complain about their costumes,  dance the waltz with a cookie that keeps dropping frosting on your feet?

Would you rather be ambushed by frosting balloons that burst raspberry goo,  gumdrops that explode into fog shaped like reindeer?

Would you rather fall into a pudding lake full of cookie crumbs  a chocolate fondue fountain that giggles every time you touch it?

Would you rather be stuck frosting cookies that keep switching places,  piping names on cupcakes that argue about spelling?

Would you rather chase a Christmas cookie that's rolling downhill, screaming "I REGRET NOTHING,"

or hide from a donut that demands its sprinkles back?

Would you rather be crowned "Snack Emperor" and forced to wear a peppermint cape,

lead a cookie choir that only sings in slow motion?

Would you rather run the cookie obstacle course wearing large fluffy reindeer Xmas slippers  judge a talent show where every cookie insists on doing magic tricks?

Would you rather have a cookie boss who only speaks through sock puppets,  work with an elf intern who thinks he's your manager and orders you to make ten million missletoe-shaped cookies?

Would you rather spend a day inside a gingerbread house that keeps shifting rooms,  sleep in one that sings lullabies with questionable lyrics?

Would you rather be slimed by raspberry filling during a cookie science experiment,  explode a gingerbread volcano filled with sour cream frosting?

Chapter 7

Nutcracker Night Patrol

At night, while the house sleeps and the snowflakes whisper, the Nutcracker Night Patrol takes charge. These toy soldiers have one mission: protect the presents at all costs. But someone gave them too much hot cocoa. Now they're suspicious of snowmen, interrogating candy canes, and treating wrapping paper like it's top secret. You've been recruited to help, but mostly to avoid getting tackled by a

Would you rather get stopped at the cookie table by a nutcracker demanding to see your snack license,  be chased down the hallway for "suspicious gift-opening vibes"?

Would you rather wear a helmet that plays trumpet sounds every time you blink,  a uniform made entirely out of leftover gift wrap?

Would you rather tiptoe across a floor covered in crinkly bows  sneak past nutcrackers practicing their "suspicious stare" in perfect unison?

Would you rather shine 50 nutcracker boots while they yell "Shinier!" in wooden voices,  brush their eyebrows with a candy cane comb?

Would you rather help a nutcracker find his missing jaw hinge  convince one that your snowman isn't a spy?

Would you rather march behind a nutcracker
who won't stop dancing,

or lead one who dramatically faints every time
someone touches a bow?

Would you rather
sneak a cookie past the
Nutcracker Cookie Guard

try to unwrap a gift
without setting off the
tinsel alarm?

Would you rather carry a backpack that jingles louder the more you lie,  wear a vest that says "Definitely Not Suspicious" in glitter letters?

Would you rather guard presents that yell "DO NOT TOUCH!" when you look at them,  ones that giggle every time you sneeze?

Would you rather join the "Super Stealth Squad" and crawl under a tree skirt,  become part of "Team Glitter Trap" and hide behind gift boxes?

Would you rather decode a secret message hidden in peppermint pieces  eat a candy cane that whispers clues in elf language?

Would you rather salute every nutcracker who passes, even the ones made of chocolate,  sing the gift-wrapping anthem every time you sneeze?

Would you rather wear night-vision goggles
that only show things in red and green,

or a sweater that screams "INTRUDER!"
if you step on wrapping paper?

Would you rather
salute a nutcracker
every time you see
your own reflection,

answer every question
with "Roger that!" even
when it's your mom?

Would you rather distract a nutcracker by reciting jokes about mistletoe  fake a sneeze so big it launches a snow globe across the room?

Would you rather crawl across a room full of jingle bells  hop from chair to chair while pretending the floor is "lava with secrets"?

Would you rather ride in a candy-cane patrol car that only goes in circles,  take notes for a nutcracker who thinks he's a reindeer?

Would you rather deliver cocoa to a nutcracker who complains about the marshmallow shape,  to one who refuses to drink unless it's stirred with a candy cane?

Would you rather climb a mountain of peppermint bark while dodging tinsel grenades,  jump rope with a string of blinking lights?

Would you rather hide under the tree
in a present costume,

or blend in by pretending to be a
very still snow globe?

Would you rather
dress up as a snowflake and
blend into the decor,  wear a pine-scented
disguise and pretend
to be a tree?

Would you rather memorize the Nutcracker Safety Handbook while using lemon-scented glitter on a Xmas card,

explain the rules to a talking teddy bear with attitude?

Would you rather translate blinking Christmas lights into secret codes

deliver messages using a kazoo that only plays holiday tunes?

Would you rather be in charge of "present surveillance" with binoculars made of candy tubes,

"snack patrol" where you taste-test cookies for safety?

Would you rather carry a sign that says "I Am Not Wrapping Paper,"

wear a giant bow that sticks to everything you touch?

Would you rather try to open a creaky door without waking the Nutcracker Guard,

escape the room by sliding across a floor covered in gift bags?

Would you rather get questioned by three nutcrackers who speak in spooky whispers,  five who all shout "SUSPICIOUS!" at the same time?

Would you rather guard the tree in a candy cane sleeping bag  sit in the lookout chair that spins wildly whenever someone says "wrapping paper"?

Would you rather earn a Nutcracker Medal of Bravery shaped like a fruitcake  sneak away quietly with your dignity and a cookie?

Would you rather end your shift glitter-covered but victorious,  still hiding under the tree because you forgot the secret nutcracker handshake?

Chapter 8:

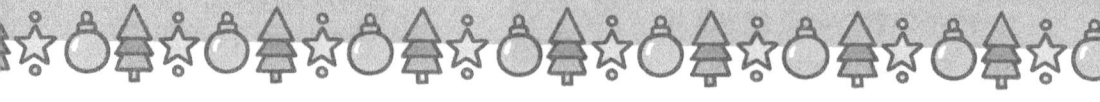

Magical Toy Malfunctions

Santa's toy-testing lab is having a full-blown meltdown. One snowman launcher blasted through the ceiling. A doll just declared herself mayor. And a musical xylophone is stuck on "Jingle Bells" and won't stop, ever. You've been called in to help the elves test the latest batch of enchanted toys. Just try not to end up glitter-glued to a rocking horse again.

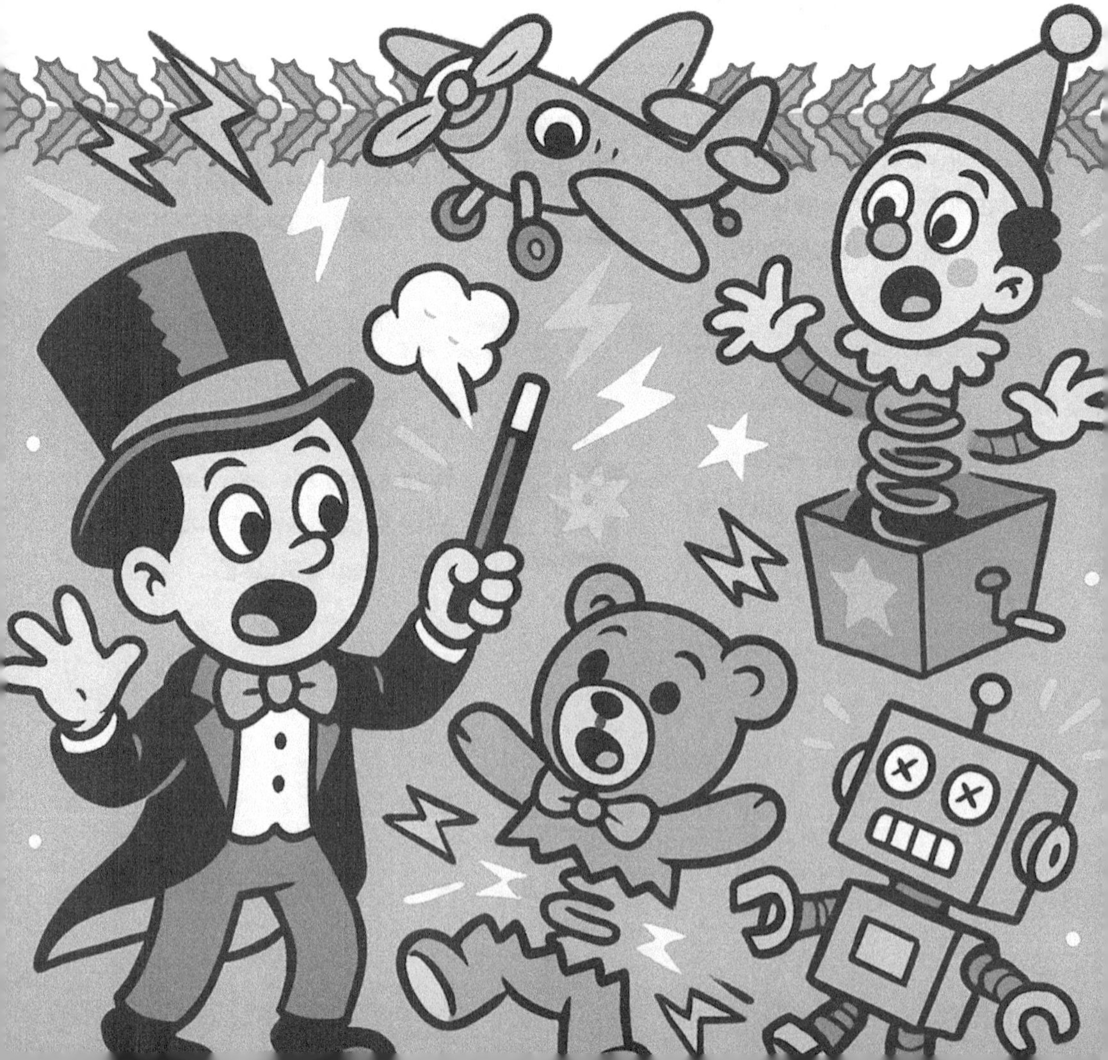

Would you rather test a toy unicorn that sneezes glitter fireworks every time it hiccups,

a robot frog that croaks "Jingle Bells" on loop until you scream?

Would you rather fix a stuffed bear that gives performance reviews like a grumpy boss,

a doll that insists on calling you "Captain Toes"?

Would you rather wear oven mitts to handle a toy dragon that breathes whipped cream,

tongs to wrangle a plush penguin with slippery dance moves?

Would you rather ride a pogo stick powered by soda fizz,

a sled that shouts "TOO FAST!" every time you turn?

Would you rather share a workbench with an elf who sneezes tinsel,

one who keeps naming the toys "Gerald" no matter what they are?

Would you rather organize a shelf of rubber ducks that sing holiday songs

alphabetize action figures that keep jumping off the shelves?

Would you rather help a gingerbread mech suit learn how to dance,

reprogram a doll that yells "POW!" every time someone blinks?

Would you rather test a snowball cannon with jammed jelly filling

a gift-wrapping machine that keeps gift-wrapping your shoes?

Would you rather play catch with a bouncy ball that never stops bouncing,

test a teddy bear that spits gumdrops when it gets excited?

Would you rather supervise an elf testing a baking set that sprays pancake batter,

one fixing a rocket sled that leaves flaming candy canes?

Would you rather test a kazoo-powered helicopter
that spins your hat off,

or a snowman launcher
that accidentally aims at Santa's cocoa mug?

Would you rather
try to fix a toy keyboard
that only types in
burp sounds,

a jack-in-the-box
that jumps out
yelling "YOGURT!"

Would you rather try to calm a nutcracker who thinks he's in charge of security,

a snow globe that sings the wrong lyrics loudly?

Would you rather power a toy train by singing Christmas carols

recharge a snowmobile by spinning in circles?

Would you rather fix a remote-control snowman who moonwalks into everything

a plush elf who insists on riding your shoulder?

Would you rather carry a bucket of rubber snakes to the inventory room

babysit a box of plush pigs that keep playing tag?

Would you rather be in charge of labeling toy boxes that won't stop moving,

sticking bows on presents that giggle when touched?

Would you rather wear winter gloves
that turn anything you touch into jelly,

or snowboots that shout compliments
when you trip?

Would you rather
wear goggles that fog up
every time an elf
yells "oops,"  ear muffs that
play reindeer snoring
on repeat?

Would you rather ride a scooter that leaves a trail of marshmallows  test a jump rope that ties itself in knots around your legs?

Would you rather stack toy boxes that keep switching labels,  organize puzzles that spell your name when finished?

Would you rather unpack a toy xylophone that only plays "Jingle Bells,"  a recorder that yells "Louder!" after every note?

Would you rather fix a toy llama that spits glitter when it's nervous,  a robot puppy that keeps chasing your shoelaces?

Would you rather test a recorder that echoes everything in slow motion,  a megaphone that adds dramatic sound effects to your voice?

Would you rather sweep the test floor
while riding a hoverboard,

or wipe toy faces with mittens
covered in syrup?

Would you rather sort
action figures that keep
sword-fighting each other  teddy bears
that fake sleep to avoid
being boxed?

Would you rather help an elf sort toys while bouncing on a trampoline,  while hopping across floor tiles that moo when stepped on?

Would you rather be chased by a toy monkey riding a wind-up sleigh,  tripped by a snowman that keeps rolling in your path?

Would you rather earn the title "Official Toy Tester" but have to wear a hat shaped like pudding,  be promoted to "Elf-in-Training" with jingle socks that never stop jingling?

Would you rather finish testing the toys but smell like burnt cocoa for a week  leave one toy behind and have it follow you, yelling, "Wait! You forgot to test me!"

Chapter 9

Candy Cane Catastrophes

It started with one candy cane. Then two. Then 4,329. Now they're everywhere, jammed in the snowblower, clogging the hot cocoa fountain, and poking out of Comet's nose (he swears it was a dare). Candy canes have officially taken over the North Pole. You've been assigned to help, but no one said anything about sticky pants or peppermint explosions.

Would you rather sit on a melted candy cane and get stuck to a chair during Santa's staff meeting,  sneeze and launch one into Mrs. Claus's pudding?

Would you rather unwrap a candy cane that smells like pickles  one that zaps your fingers with a peppermint fizz every time you touch it?

Would you rather ride a scooter made of candy canes that squeaks "WHEEE!" when you turn,  a sled that sprays mint mist and fogs your goggles?

Would you rather grow a candy cane mustache every time someone says "Merry,"  eyebrows that twinkle red and green whenever you're nervous?

Would you rather wear peppermint socks that crunch with every step and wake up the sleeping reindeer,  gloves that jingle wildly whenever you wave?

Would you rather ride a flying candy cane
that spins like a blender,

or one that honks "HO HO WHOA!"
every time you blink?

Would you rather be
crowned "Candy Cane
Captain" and lead a parade
in a wrapper-cape that
sticks to your knees,

join the Cleanup Crew
with a mop
that sprays peppermint
when it's mad?

Would you rather wake up with candy canes stuffed in your slippers  find one taped to your toothbrush with a note from "Santa's Elf Surveillance Team"?

Would you rather brush your teeth with a cinnamon candy cane that burns your tongue a little,  floss with tinsel that tickles your brain?

Would you rather step barefoot on a crushed candy cane and yelp like a reindeer,  find one melted inside your snow boot halfway through sled duty?

Would you rather show up to elf karaoke night with a candy cane stuck in your hair  glued to your pants during your solo?

Would you rather decorate a gingerbread house with candy canes that yell "WRONG SPOT!" every time you stick them,  ones that snap in half and cry about it?

Would you rather get chased by
squirrels after dropping candy cane crumbs,

or be followed by a snowman who thinks
you're made of sugar?

Would you rather
get caught sword-fighting a
nutcracker with
a candy cane

jousting elves in the
hallway right as
Santa walks in?

Would you rather discover your snowball launcher is jammed with sticky candy canes,  your cocoa filled with crushed peppermint and jingle bell glitter?

Would you rather play hide-and-seek in a forest of giant candy canes that squeak when touched,  chase a runaway one yelling, "TOO SWEET TO CATCH ME!"

Would you rather build a candy cane ladder that bends like spaghetti,  stack them into a throne for an elf who insists he's royalty?

Would you rather hiccup mini candy canes every time someone tells a joke,  burp peppermint fog that makes the elves giggle uncontrollably?

Would you rather carry a backpack full of sticky candy canes that keep falling out in the toy lab,  pull a wagon shaped like a peppermint pig that keeps snorting?

Would you rather build a snowman
with a candy cane nose that keeps falling off,

or give it candy cane arms that wave
every time someone walks by?

Would you rather
be wrapped in blinking
candy cane lights that play
jingles when you move,  stuck to wrapping paper
with elf-grade
peppermint glue?

Would you rather trip on a candy cane and knock over the hot cocoa tower,  slip into a pile of marshmallows and take three elves with you?

Would you rather hiccup and launch a candy cane into the wreath Santa just finished hanging,  into your supervisor elf's cocoa during inspection?

Would you rather build a snow fort with candy cane fences that collapse in a minty mess  defend it using a peppermint launcher that jams every time it gets windy?

Would you rather be trapped in a sleigh seat covered in peppermint goo,  in a supply closet where the candy canes keep sticking to your socks?

Would you rather eat a candy cane that turns your tongue bright blue for a day,  one that makes your voice sound like an elf every time you laugh?

Would you rather be the official candy cane taste-tester and try 47 flavors in one day,  the "unsticker" of candy canes from all the reindeer hooves?

Would you rather wear peppermint boots that shout "HOLIDAY MODE: ACTIVATE!" when you run,  a scarf that smells like cocoa and hums "Deck the Halls"?

Would you rather accidentally drop a candy cane into the sleigh engine and hear it sputter "Oops,"  open your lunchbox to find it packed with nothing but peppermint sticks?

Would you rather end the day covered head to toe in candy cane goo but be named a holiday hero,  stay squeaky clean but have to scrub the cocoa fountain for a week?

Chapter 10

North Pole Tech Fail

Santa upgraded the sleigh's Smart System, and now nothing works right. The reindeer GPS keeps yelling "Recalculating!" in four languages, the wrapping machine won't stop singing opera, and the Nice List got erased and replaced with a pizza menu. Whoever designed this update definitely never tested it in a snowstorm.

Would you rather ride in Santa's sleigh while it only understands Penguin  try to reboot it by humming "Jingle Bells" backward?

Would you rather fix an elf printer that spits out gingerbread emojis nonstop  explain to Santa why the sleigh now thinks it's a sandwich?

Would you rather help elves update their phones using candy-corn chargers  plug in a tangled mess of lights that shock you with static?

Would you rather restart the Nice List app before it replaces everyone's name with pasta  fix a frozen screen using a peppermint stick?

Would you rather type on a keyboard that adds glitter to every word  wear gloves that gift-wrap everything you touch?

Would you rather
wear a coat that reads
your texts out loud in
Santa's voice

boots that bark
when you walk?

Would you rather
ride a robot reindeer
with the hiccups

get chased by
a snow drone
that won't stop recording?

Would you rather
reset the sleigh's GPS while
it's flying sideways

try to stop
a wrapping robot that
wrapped the couch?

Would you rather
be zapped by a candy cane
charging cable

accidentally
download the Fruitcake
Operating System?

Would you rather
fix Santa's belt that
now shouts "Ho Ho NO!"
every 30 seconds

a snow machine
that launches
marshmallows?

Would you rather press the glowing "Fix Everything" button
and hope for the best

or hand the controls over
to the Yeti?

Would you rather
fix a toy app
that keeps crashing

ride a hover-present
that randomly
launches into walls?

Would you rather get glitter-blasted by a toy unicorn  caught in a bubble storm from a sleigh horn that thinks it's a spa?

Would you rather reboot a voice assistant that sings opera  stop the sleigh from texting your mom every time it moves?

Would you rather control the toy machine with a pudding-powered joystick  a glitter-spewing steering wheel?

Would you rather deal with a Nice List that's stuck on "loading..."  fix a printer that only prints upside-down maps?

Would you rather program a snowball launcher with your nose  balance on a tablet that plays ice skating videos on loop?

Would you rather type
using gingerbread mittens

or shout at a robot elf that's ignoring you
through noise-canceling earmuffs?

Would you rather
translate reindeer messages
filled with carrot emojis

delete 3,000
elf selfies from the
workshop's cloud?

Would you rather fix a drone that sings "Deck the Halls" in chipmunk voices  one that drops tinsel every time it spins?

Would you rather update a sleigh system that only runs on banana peels  a translator that switches English to pirate talk?

Would you rather fix the gift-sorting robot that judges presents by how squishy they are  the sleigh horn that only plays fart sounds?

Would you rather use a frozen candy keyboard that melts as you type  a snow globe mouse that keeps spinning away?

Would you rather be trapped inside an elf's playlist full of yodeling  watch Santa try to code using jellybeans?

Would you rather wear a smartwatch
that calls you "Grandma"

or elf glasses that turn everything
into dancing candy?

Would you rather
clean up after a frosting-
exploding snowman app

remove confetti from
Santa's beard after a
surprise selfie blast?

Would you rather ride a sleigh that moonwalks  reset a system that adds everyone to the Naughty List when they sneeze?

Would you rather fix a snowflake-shaped laptop with sticky buttons  a cocoa-powered phone that only sends reindeer GIFs?

Would you rather wear a jacket that accidentally live-streams everything you say  a hat that mishears you and orders 400 pineapples?

Would you rather get stuck in a holiday slideshow of Santa's baby photos  fix a snow globe projector that won't stop spinning?

Chapter 11

Yeti at the Front Door

One morning, someone knocked on Santa's front door. Big feet. Big smile. Bigger appetite. A yeti! He says he's here to "help with Christmas," but so far, all he's done is clog the cocoa machine with snowballs and nap in the gift-wrapping station. You've been assigned to keep him out of trouble... good luck.

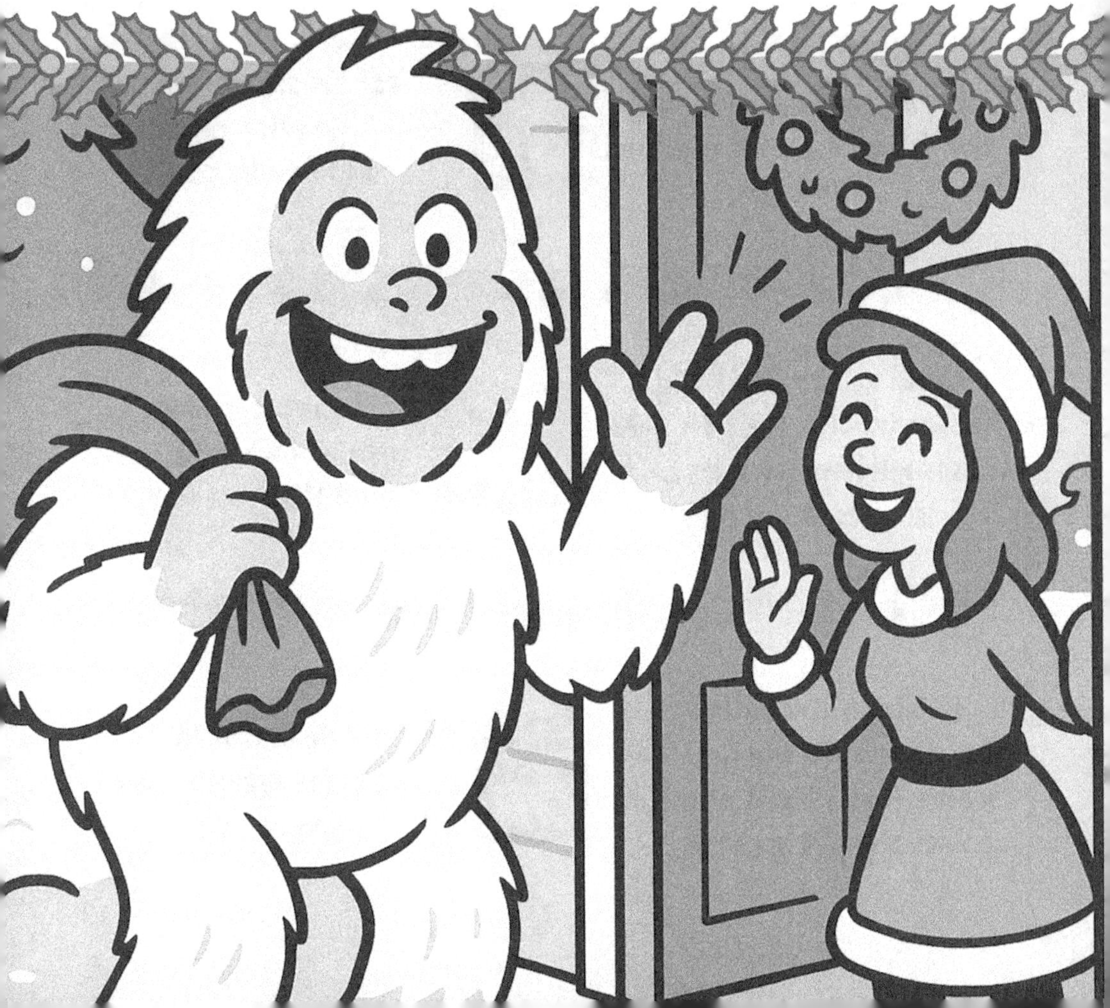

Would you rather teach the Yeti how to wrap presents, even though he keeps taping his hands to the boxes,  help him carry gifts while he accidentally sits on them?

Would you rather go sledding with the yeti, who yells "YETI POWER!" the whole way,  play tag with him, even though he thinks every tag is a wrestling move?

Would you rather share your sandwich with the Yeti who thinks mustard is lip balm,  eat his special snack: frozen pickles and candy canes?

Would you rather build a snowman with the yeti, who uses mittens for eyes and jellybeans for ears,  decorate cookies with him while he eats all the frosting?

Would you rather ice skate with the yeti, who wears fuzzy boots and falls every five seconds,  ride in a sleigh he keeps steering into snowbanks?

Would you rather let the Yeti decorate the Christmas tree
with spaghetti and socks,

or be in charge of sweeping up after
he shakes snow out of his fur indoors?

Would you rather
teach the yeti to use the
gift scanner that keeps
calling him "Grandma,"  try fixing the
elf walkie-talkie
he glued to a banana?

Would you rather play hide-and-seek with a yeti who hides behind candy canes and still sticks out,  play charades with one who only acts out "yeti"?

Would you rather be on cocoa patrol while the Yeti dumps 47 marshmallows into every mug,  sit next to him during caroling while he sings off-key and throws confetti?

Would you rather clean up the cookie decorating mess the Yeti made with sprinkles in your shoes,  vacuum marshmallows off the ceiling after his "cocoa experiment"?

Would you rather wear the yeti's fuzzy scarf that smells like old waffles,  lend him your mittens and get them back full of snowflakes and raisins?

Would you rather help the Yeti make reindeer snacks and accidentally feed them jellybeans,  organize presents by color and end up with a giant pile of "mostly purple"?

Would you rather go on a snowball mission with the yeti who throws snowballs the size of pumpkins,

or build a fort together
that he accidentally squashes while dancing?

Would you rather ride the candy train with the yeti and he eats half the track  try fitting both of you in the same sleigh seat for movie night?

Would you rather help the yeti untangle Christmas lights he used as shoelaces  fix the sleigh horn he replaced with a rubber chicken?

Would you rather race the Yeti down a snowy hill where he rolls like a snow boulder,  play hopscotch on peppermint ice cubes with him?

Would you rather wear a Santa hat that the yeti accidentally sat on,  let him borrow your coat and get it back smelling like hot cocoa and mystery meat?

Would you rather be in charge of elf yoga with the Yeti doing loud sit-ups,  play musical chairs where he keeps sitting on the chair?

Would you rather help the yeti sort letters to Santa while he keeps sniffing the envelopes,  organize the toy shelf after he builds a tower out of rubber ducks?

Would you rather wear matching pajamas
with the Yeti that are two sizes too big,

or matching slippers
that honk every time you step?

Would you rather
be the yeti's partner in the
elf dance-off,  on his team in the
Great Snowball Relay
(he forgets how to pass)?

Would you rather teach the yeti to say "Happy Holidays" without sneezing glitter,  let him lead a caroling group with a kazoo and no clue?

Would you rather take the yeti to reindeer school, where he tries to fly,  to the toy-testing lab where he thinks everything is a squeaky toy?

Would you rather help the Yeti fill stockings, but he stuffs them with carrots and glue sticks,  wrap gifts while he keeps sticking bows to your forehead?

Would you rather decorate gingerbread houses with the Yeti who uses whipped cream for wallpaper,  build snow forts while he keeps licking the walls?

Would you rather keep the yeti from falling into the hot cocoa tub  explain to Santa why he turned the Naughty List into a paper airplane?

Would you rather try teaching the Yeti North Pole manners,  make up a new job for him so he stops "helping" in the mailroom?

Would you rather follow the yeti around with a mop  chase him with a lint roller after his fur explodes in the wind?

Would you rather have the Yeti as your holiday sidekick and never be bored again,  trade him back to the mountains in exchange for a snow-cone machine?

Would you rather let the Yeti stay for Christmas and sleep in the gift closet,  send him home with a sled full of fruitcake and a hug that lasts three minutes?

Chapter 12:

Caroling Chaos —
The Musical Meltdown Finale

The big holiday performance is tonight, and everything that could go wrong already has. The elf choir lost their voices from too much peppermint bark. The reindeer keep dancing out of sync. And someone gave the Yeti a tambourine. Now you're center stage, trying to lead a musical finale that won't turn into a total snowball disaster.

Would you rather sing a solo while your nose lights up like Rudolph's,  while your voice randomly squeaks like a rubber duck?

Would you rather wear a holiday sweater that unravels mid-performance,  jingle bell shoes that won't stop jingling... even during the silent part?

Would you rather lead a carol where the elves forget the lyrics and just hum awkwardly,  one where they sing everything two beats too early?

Would you rather be in the elf dance line but keep spinning into the curtains,  in the gingerbread chorus where half the cookies crumble mid-song?

Would you rather hold the music sheets that keep blowing away,  try to keep your hat from flopping over your eyes every time you bow?

Would you rather
sing backup for a penguin
trio who only know one note,  for nutcrackers
who turn their heads
instead of clapping?

Would you rather
trip over the mic cord and
land in the cocoa tub,  slip on tinsel and
land in the front row?

Would you rather
perform wearing antlers
that blink with every word,  a scarf that
wraps tighter every time
you sing too loudly?

Would you rather
lead the finale while
hiccuping marshmallows  while accidentally
shouting the wrong lyrics at
the top of your lungs?

Would you rather
perform with mittens that
clap on their own,  a hat that blasts
"Jingle Bells" every time
you turn your head?

Would you rather sing with your mouth
full of candy canes

or try to dance in
marshmallow-stuffed boots?

Would you rather
ring the triangle but
accidentally poke yourself
every time,

play the jingle bells that
launch across the room
when you shake them?

Would you rather get a surprise snowball confetti shower during your solo,  have a spotlight that follows the wrong person the whole time?

Would you rather sing your part while riding a spinning gift box  while sliding back and forth on peppermint ice?

Would you rather start the song too early and finish alone,  start late and run to catch up while singing super fast?

Would you rather fall into the props table and land in a pile of wrapping paper,  bump the snow machine and get blasted with flurries?

Would you rather hold a note so long your face turns red,  miss your cue and shout, "Cherry Mistmas!" instead of "Merry Christmas!"

Would you rather
get tangled in ribbon mid-dance,

or knock over the elf orchestra
with a flying candy cane?

Would you rather
wear pants that squeak
with every step,

boots that light up
like fireworks
when you jump?

Would you rather share a microphone with the Yeti who burps between verses,  a reindeer who only sings in moos?

Would you rather wear a tutu made of tinsel that squeaks,  a cape that gets caught in everything?

Would you rather have your song echo loudly every time you say "snow,"  turn into bubble sounds whenever you say "Santa"?

Would you rather hit the high note perfectly and fall into a pile of gift bows,  hit the wrong note but make the audience laugh and cheer?

Would you rather end the show by slipping on stage and landing with a SPLAT,  by sneezing into the conductor's beard?

Would you rather take a bow and accidentally
knock down the snowman set,

or wave so hard your hat flies
into the crowd?

Would you rather
get glitter-stormed
during the grand finale,  get lifted on a sleigh
by elves who forget
the ending pose?

Would you rather lead the elf choir, even though they all have hiccups,  direct the reindeer band where every instrument sounds like farts?

Would you rather close the curtain and trip over the yeti's tail,  get a standing ovation followed by a whipped cream pie to the face?

Would you rather be carried off stage by a penguin parade chanting your name,  get a candy trophy and accidentally eat half of it?

Would you rather keep the party going with one more musical mess-up  end the show by falling into a snowdrift of laughter?

⋆ Enjoyed The Adventure? ⋆

If this book made you laugh, cringe (in the best way), or shout "EW, NO WAY!" at least once ,
we'd love to hear about it!

Reviews help more families discover the fun, and they let us know what kind of silly chaos to cook up next time.

Even a short review makes a huge difference!

If you're reading this with a grown-up, maybe you can ask them to help leave a review on Amazon. Just a sentence or two is perfect.

Thanks for being part of this merry mess.

You're the real MVP of the North Pole.

☀ You Made It! ☀

If you've reached this page, that means you survived dancing elves, exploding candy canes, and a yeti who thought snowballs were snacks. Nice work!

We hope you had some laughs, made weird faces, and maybe even got into a few debates with your friends or family over the wildest "Would You Rather" choices.

You've officially earned the title of **North Pole Chaos Champion.** Not everyone can handle this much holiday mayhem.

Before you go, here's one last question:

Would you rather...
Put this book away until next Christmas?
Or...
Flip back to your favorite chapter and play it all over again?

Whatever you choose, thanks for being part of the fun. And remember: if you ever see a reindeer in sunglasses or a snowman doing jazz hands...
You might still be in the game.

About Riddleland

Riddleland is a mum + dad run publishing company. We are passionate about creating fun and innovative books to help children develop their reading skills and fall in love with reading. If you have suggestions for us or want to work with us, shoot us an email at

riddleland@riddlelandforkids.com

Our family's favorite quote:

"Creativity is an area in which younger people have a tremendous advantage since they have an endearing habit of always questioning past wisdom and authority."

~ Bill Hewlett

www.ingramcontent.com/pod-product-compliance
Lightning Source LLC
Chambersburg PA
CBHW061659120626
46550CB00003B/1009